DEAF PEOPLE
IN HEARING WORLDS

UNIT 7
WHOSE WELFARE?

PREPARED FOR THE COURSE TEAM BY
LYNNE HAWCROFT, ON BEHALF OF THE
ROYAL NATIONAL INSTITUTE FOR THE DEAF

WITH CONTRIBUTIONS FROM TIM DANT
(SECTIONS 4.1, 4.2 AND 4.3) AND
DAVID MOORHEAD (SECTION 5)

PAINTING ON COVER AND TITLE PAGE BY TREVOR LANDELL

THIS COURSE HAS BEEN PRODUCED WITH FUNDING
FROM THE DEPARTMENT OF HEALTH

D251 Core Course Team

ANNE DARBY Diploma Placements Officer, Faculty of Social Sciences

SUSAN GREGORY Senior Lecturer in Psychology, Faculty of Social Sciences (Course Team Chair)

YVONNE HOLMES Secretary, Faculty of Social Sciences

LINDA JANES Course Manager, Faculty of Social Sciences

GEORGE TAYLOR Lecturer in Interdisciplinary Social Sciences, Faculty of Social Sciences

Other Open University Contributors

JULIET BISHOP Research Fellow in Social Sciences, Faculty of Social Sciences

DEBBIE CROUCH Designer

TIM DANT Research Fellow in Health and Social Welfare, Continuing Education

VIC FINKELSTEIN Senior Lecturer in Health and Social Welfare, Continuing Education

GERALD HALES Research Fellow, Institute of Educational Technology

FIONA HARRIS Editor

KEITH HOWARD Graphic Artist

MARY JOHN Senior Lecturer in Psychology, Faculty of Social Sciences

VIC LOCKWOOD BBC Producer

KEN PATTON BBC Producer

ALISON TUCKER BBC Producer

External Consultants

LORNA ALLSOP Centre for Deaf Studies, University of Bristol

LARAINE CALLOW Consultant in Deafness

MARY FIELDER National Council of Social Workers with Deaf People

GILLIAN M. HARTLEY Teacher, Thorn Park School, Bradford

LYNNE HAWCROFT Royal National Institute for the Deaf

JIM KYLE Centre for Deaf Studies, University of Bristol

PADDY LADD London Deaf Video Project

CARLO LAURENZI National Deaf Children's Society

CLIVE MASON Presenter, BBC 'See Hear'

RUKHSANA MEHERALI Educational Psychologist, Royal School for the Deaf, Derby

DOROTHY MILES Writer, Lecturer and Poet

BOB PECKFORD British Deaf Association

CHRISTINE PLAYER Tutor Adviser

SHARON RIDGEWAY National Council of Social Workers with Deaf People

JANICE SILO Teacher of the Deaf, Derbyshire

External Assessors

MARY BRENNAN Co-director, MA and Advanced Diploma in Sign Language Studies, University of Durham

MALCOLM PAYNE Head of Department of Applied Community Studies, Manchester Polytechnic

Sign Language Interpreters

BYRON CAMPBELL

ELIZABETH JONES

KYRA POLLITT

LINDA RICHARDS

The Open University
Walton Hall, Milton Keynes
MK7 6AB

First published 1991

Designed by the Graphic Design Group of the Open University

Printed in the United Kingdom by The Open University

ISBN 0 7492 0053 7

This publication forms part of the Open University course D251 Issues in Deafness. If you have not enrolled on the course and would like to buy this or other Open University material, please write to Open University Educational Enterprises Ltd, 12 Cofferidge Close, Stony Stratford, Milton Keynes MK11 1BY, United Kingdom. If you wish to enquire about enrolling as an Open University student, please write to the Admissions Office, The Open University, P.O. Box 48, Walton Hall, Milton Keynes MK7 6AB, United Kingdom.

Unit 7 Whose Welfare?

prepared for the course team by Lynne Hawcroft on behalf of The Royal National Institute for the Deaf, with contributions from Tim Dant (Sections 4.1, 4.2 and 4.3) and David Moorhead (Section 5)

Contents

Associated study materials

Reader Two, Article 6.6, 'A Stimulus to Learning, A Measure of Ability', T. Stewart Simpson.

Reader Two, Article 7.1, 'The Development of Local Voluntary Societies for Adult Deaf Persons in England', Kenneth Lysons.

continued

Reader Two, Article 7.2, 'Deaf People, Ethnic Minorities and Social Policy', George Taylor.

Reader Two, Article 7.3, 'The State, Social Work and Deafness', David Parratt and Brenda Tipping.

Reader Two, Article 7.4, 'Sign Language Interpreting: An Emerging Profession', Liz Scott-Gibson.

Reader Two, Article 7.5, 'Social Work and Interpreting', David Moorhead.

Reader Two, Article 7.6, ' "We" Are Not Disabled, "You" Are', Vic Finkelstein.

Reader Two, Article 7.7, 'Deaf People and Minority Groups in the UK', Jim Kyle.

Legislation Booklet

D251 Issues in Deafness

Unit 1   *Perspectives on Deafness: An Introduction*

Block 1   Being Deaf
Unit 2   *The Deaf Community*
Unit 3   *British Sign Language, Communication and Deafness*
Unit 4   *The Other Deaf Community?*

Block 2   Deaf People in Hearing Worlds
Unit 5   *Education and Deaf People: Learning to Communicate or Communicating to Learn?*
Unit 6   *The Manufacture of Disadvantage*
Unit 7   *Whose Welfare?*

Block 3   Constructing Deafness
Unit 8   *The Social Construction of Deafness*
Unit 9   *Deaf People as a Minority Group: The Political Process*
Unit 10   *Deaf Futures*

Readers
Reader One: Taylor, G. and Bishop, J. (eds) (1990) *Being Deaf: The Experience of Deafness*, London, Pinter Publishers.
Reader Two: Gregory, S. and Hartley, G.M. (eds) (1990) *Constructing Deafness*, London, Pinter Publishers.

Set Books
Kyle, J. and Woll, B. (1985) *Sign Language: The Study of Deaf People and Their Language*, Cambridge, Cambridge University Press.
Miles, D. (1988) *British Sign Language: A Beginner's Guide*, London, BBC Books (BBC Enterprises). With a chapter by Paddy Ladd.

Videotapes
Video One   *Sandra's Story: The History of a Deaf Family*
Video Two   *Sign Language*
Video Three   *Deaf People and Mental Health*
Video Four   *Signs of Change: Politics and the Deaf Community*

Objectives

After studying this unit students should be able to:

1   Describe the context in which social work with Deaf people is provided.
2   Understand some of the historical influences which have shaped present day services.
3   Appreciate the views, held by Deaf people, of social workers.
4   Understand the basic issues relating to social work and interpreting.
5   Begin to make links from social work with Deaf people to social work in general and into broader policy areas.
6   Recognize the common theme of professional power described in other units and relate it to social work with Deaf people.
7   Be alerted to the major changes due to be implemented in the 1990s.

Study guide

The unit divides into three topics and we suggest you take one part each week, reading it through quickly first to familiarize yourself with its contents, and then reading it more systematically, undertaking the activities and consulting the suggested Reader articles and relevant sections of the *Legislation Booklet.*

Week one

Objectives
Introduction
Section 1 'The development of social work with Deaf people'
Legislation Booklet
Reader Two, Article 7.1 by Kenneth Lysons

Week two

Section 2 'Interpreting'
Reader Two, Article 7.4 by Liz Scott-Gibson
Reader Two, Article 7.5 by David Moorhead
Reader Two , Article 6.6 by T. Stewart Simpson
Section 3 'The role of Deaf people'
Reader Two, Article 7.6 by Vic Finkelstein
Reader Two, Article 7.7 by Jim Kyle

Week three

Section 4 'Social work provision'
Reader Two, Article 7.2 by George Taylor
Reader Two, Article 7.3 by David Parratt and Brenda Tipping
Section 5, 'Back to the future'
Section 6, Conclusion

You should also have time in week three to review the unit as a whole.

Introduction

This unit, located in the block *Deaf People in Hearing Worlds*, introduces you to the uniquely powerful position social workers have in relation to Deaf people. In common with other professional groups such as teachers, social workers influence Deaf people's lives by providing access to services they may require. However, this unit will demonstrate how the role of the social worker is particularly crucial, being a gate-keeping role for a wide range of services, many of which lie outside of social services. The unit will trace some of the historical events which have shaped this relationship and how Deaf people relate to the hearing world of welfare. For example, in the past, contact between the police, doctors, many other professionals and Deaf people would have involved a social worker acting as adviser, facilitator, interpreter or a combination of these. This resulted in social workers operating in many interview situations not related to social work or social services duties. The unit will briefly touch on the world of social work in general, as well as work with Deaf people, and trace some of the developments which are influencing change in this area of work.

A number of major themes underpin this unit and link it to the other units you have already worked through, including:

1   The way in which society views Deaf people is reflected in legislation and institutions and these have generally failed to take account of Deaf people as a distinct group with their own culture and language. This lack of recognition has resulted in Deaf people being hidden within the general label of disability. This has meant that even in those agencies which supposedly directly serve people with disabilities, such as social services departments, the particular needs of Deaf people have been largely ignored. Within social services departments Social Workers with Deaf People are often marginalized and have little opportunity to influence decision making. This produces an interesting paradox in that the professionals who appear all powerful in relation to Deaf people are, in turn, relatively powerless within their own organizations.

2   The pervading power of social workers in Deaf people's lives is related to their role as interpreters/communicators between Deaf people and the hearing world. Outside of direct family and friends, social workers have been the only state professionals who have seen the necessity to acquire

sign language skills in order to do their job effectively. All social workers exercise powers invested in them by the state, such as the power to remove children from their families in certain circumstances. In this respect, Social Workers with Deaf People have a more powerful position than their social work colleagues by virtue of their bridging and gatekeeping role.

3   In contrast to other professional groups, such as doctors and teachers, Social Workers with Deaf People are the only professional group which has consistently believed that social work must be provided through the language of the service user. Despite difficulties in achieving adequate sign language standards, they are the only group to attempt to provide a professional service using sign language over many years. This belief has caused the social work profession many struggles, not only because sign language skills have not been valued within their agencies, but also because major trends such as integration have swept through agencies, buffeting Social Workers with Deaf People along the way. As you study this unit, you will see that Social Workers with Deaf People have, just, retained the specialist area of work, but this is under threat from very low recruitment and lack of specialist training, and is about to be swept along in the latest maelstrom of changes affecting social services departments as they enter the 1990s.

As very little is written about Social Workers with Deaf People in this country and hard data on their circumstances are very scarce, there will be few direct references in the unit to major written accounts. Of course, this reflects not only the scarcity of workers with Deaf people and the struggle that they have to survive, but also the scant attention that is shown to this area of work, by either local or central government agencies. The unit will rely heavily on Reader articles and will make much more use of the author's personal experience than is usual. Equally, the views of Deaf people on social work have rarely been documented and so individual views and anecdotes will replace a broader perspective, except in this Introduction in the section 'The 1880 view', which is based on a meeting of Deaf people organized by a debating group to supply The Open University course team with their views on social work. This group made valid and fascinating comments which are discussed in the unit, but students should remember that Deaf people are no more likely to hold the same views about any subject than the rest of us, and so the views they expressed should not be taken as universal.

How the unit works

We start by looking at the Report of the 1880 Group, a debating society of Deaf people. We do this because it gives us an initial focus on the views of Deaf people as expressed in a similar way in Units 5 and 6, and it indicates the issues which will be discussed later in this unit. Many of the issues will be briefly touched upon here but as they will be looked at more fully later in this unit, you do not need to worry if this section leaves you with lots of unanswered questions: that is the intention. Following the discussion in this Introduction, Section 1 traces work with deaf people to its voluntary society origins, and we look at the present place of local voluntary organizations in providing services. The current state of social work with Deaf people is outlined, with a brief look at what social workers do and whether this is comparable to social work in general. While it is not easy to define social work, we shall take as a working definition and starting point the description offered by the Central Council for Education and Training in Social Work (CCETSW):

> 1.1 Social work is an accountable professional activity which enables individuals, families and groups to identify personal, social and environmental difficulties adversely affecting them. Social work enables them to manage these difficulties through supportive, rehabilitative, protective or corrective action. Social work promotes social welfare and responds to wider social needs promoting equal opportunities for every age, gender, sexual preference, class, disability, race, culture and creed. Social work has the responsibility to protect the vulnerable and exercise authority under statute.

> 1.2 Social workers are part of a network of welfare, health, criminal justice and penal provision. They have a responsibility to ensure proper use of the resources available to them. Parliament lays down the legal framework and delineates the powers of statutory, voluntary and private agencies within which social workers practise. Their role can vary in residential, day care, domiciliary, fieldwork and community settings, but they share a common core of knowledge, skills and values.

> (CCETSW, 1989)

In Section 2, recent developments to separate the various aspects of social work with Deaf people into distinct roles will be examined and will focus on one major area, that of interpreting. The symbiotic existence of social work and interpreting is now changing and the resulting separation will be traced. We shall use the description 'interpreter' to apply to anybody undertaking the interpreting role. Strictly, the term should only be applied to registered interpreters, and those not registered should be known as 'communicators'. However, in practice, it is not always possible to differentiate and, therefore, for simplicity we shall use the term 'interpreter' in a general sense.

Section 3 looks at the role of Deaf people in social work. The underlying theme of this section is the contribution that Deaf people could make to service provision and the major role that social workers who are Deaf themselves could take in shaping future services, alongside service users. This parallels the roles of Deaf teachers and Deaf mental health workers that you will have read about in Units 5 and 6.

Section 4 begins a process of stepping back from social work with Deaf people and looking at the broader context. It examines the place of work with Deaf people in social work generally and you may be surprised that this was not dealt with much earlier. However, by this point in the unit you will appreciate the important influence of the missioners and the voluntary organizations on the establishment of the specialist role. This situation is, of course, not static and may now be changing so that social workers who enter the work with Deaf people without any prior contact with deafness, but with previous experience in social work, may well identify themselves much more with the general field.

The final section speculates on the major changes that are about to take place in the 1990s following the National Health Service and Community Care Act, and begins to consider the possible impact of these changes on the place of Deaf services in the future.

The 1880 view

> People felt that many of the problems connected with social work were based on fundamental misconceptions of Deaf people.
>
> (Notes of a meeting of the 1880 Group, 1989)

The 1880 Group, a London-based debating society of Deaf people, held an open meeting in 1989 to consider the need for Social Workers with Deaf People. They resolved that there should be Social Workers with Deaf People, but that major changes were required to improve their appreciation of Deaf culture and their communication skills and also in the recruitment, training and deployment of such workers. The misconceptions referred to by the group were, they felt, related to the failure of social workers to demonstrate their acceptance of the importance of the Deaf community in their work with Deaf people. They suggested this resulted in the following problems:

Δ   the poor use of British Sign Language (BSL), especially in receptive skills;

Δ   the inappropriate use of generic social workers;

Δ   inaccessibility outside office hours;

Δ   Deaf people viewed as a 'problem' rather than as a distinct minority group;

Δ   decisions made by senior staff in social services, without any involvement of Deaf people.

Let us consider this list of problems which the 1880 Group suggested resulted from social workers' misconceptions and examine these further.

The poor use of BSL

The low level of skill in using BSL is a common complaint levelled at social workers in recent years and was confirmed officially in the Social Services Inspectorate report *Say It Again* (DHSS, 1988). It is often suggested that when services were primarily provided by local voluntary organizations, the opportunity to mix with Deaf people was greater and that by living as part of the Deaf community the missioner/welfare officer was able to develop high levels of fluency. It is difficult to make comparisons as there were no national standards available to measure skill competency until the establishment of the Council for Advancement of Communication with Deaf People (CACDP) in 1980. Is it possible recollections are clouded by nostalgia? It may be that recent advances in the establishment of training and examination have revealed the inadequacies in language skills more starkly and who knows how the earlier workers would have faired if they had been subject to the same scrutiny.

The inappropriate use of generic social workers

The second point on the 1880 Group list refers to the existence of generic social workers, and their inability to provide appropriate services to Deaf people. This may refer to those authorities which do not employ any specialist workers at all, of which there were fourteen in 1988 (RNID, 1988), or where there are so few specialists that other workers have to work directly with Deaf people. It may also refer to the practice of some Social Workers with Deaf People, being unable or unwilling to undertake certain areas of work. The absence of specialist social workers makes it difficult for authorities to fulfil their statutory duties satisfactorily. Those authorities without any specialist workers at all, for example, are likely to try to 'muddle through', by a combination of gesture, speech and writing, in their everyday dealing with Deaf people. Deaf people, quite rightly, complain that this is totally unacceptable and shows a blatant disregard for their needs. In certain high-risk areas of work—for example, mental health assessment— some of these departments would attempt to bring in expertise from outside their own authority. Even if they try to do this, however, they will often be unable to find an appropriate person, because of the shortage of both social workers and interpreters and the lack of formal systems to locate them or ensure an adequate level of competence. The use of freelance interpreters is increasing, but caution needs to be exercised in doing so in highly complex professional tasks for which they may have had no training or preparation.

Some Deaf people may have approached social services departments employing specialist workers only to find that these workers would not always be available to them. This could be due simply to shortage of personnel, and if departments only employ one or two specialist workers then they may not have the time to see every Deaf person who approaches them. Also, as we will see later, many more people working as Social Workers with Deaf People are unqualified in social work than are their generic colleagues and this bars them from certain areas of work—for example, arranging compulsory admission for psychiatric treatment under the Mental Health Act 1983 (see the *Legislation Booklet*).

This is amply illustrated in the case of a Deaf woman who was admitted against her will to a psychiatric hospital under the Mental Health Act. Neither the psychiatrist nor the social worker were able to communicate with the Deaf woman who used BSL. Her family had asked for her admission. To their credit, the professionals asked for an interpreter, and obtained a freelance interpreter who was a native BSL user. You may, therefore, make the assumption that the situation was dealt with adequately, although you perhaps would have wished the doctor and social worker to have had better skills themselves. In fact, the woman was detained illegally, and was later released, because the interpreter was not skilled in mental health terminology and so failed to convey precise information. The question remains, would Deaf people prefer a social worker with high level communication skills, to an interpreter trained in distinct settings, such as mental health, working with professionals expert in their own area? This question will remain unanswered until there are more social workers and interpreters available, so that real comparisons can be made. This is discussed in more detail in Section 2.

◀ Activity 1
(a) Write down a short list of situations in which you feel a social worker and not an interpreter would be appropriate.

(b) Write down a short list of situations in which you feel an interpreter and not a social worker would be appropriate. ◀

Inaccessibility outside office hours — Interpreter instead

The third problem mentioned by the 1880 Group was the availability of social workers outside office hours. This may relate to an earlier age when more social workers/missioners were part of the Deaf community. Do the majority of Deaf people really want to contact a social worker with any frequency, either inside or outside office hours, or do they want access to information and interpreting which are presently locked into the social work role? Most social services departments do provide an emergency service out of office hours and many of these have back-up from Social Workers with Deaf People. However, in the author's experience, the majority of call-outs involve interpreting in police and medical settings and only rarely are workers dealing with social service tasks. This raises the question of the inappropriate use of social services personnel and will be discussed more fully later.

Deaf people viewed as a 'problem' rather than as a distinct minority group

As you have seen in previous units, professionals and the agencies which employ them define their service users into 'problem groups'. Social workers are no different in this respect and so their response to Deaf people is as a 'helper'. The 1880 Group properly linked this stance to the training of social workers, which concentrates on client groups and 'their' problems. It may well be more positive to enable workers to view Deaf people as a minority group; however, there is little evidence to suggest that minority groups receive any better service from social workers than Deaf people do. If this view is part of a political movement to locate Deaf people differently and to remove them from the all-encompassing net of welfare, it is understandable, but would it lead to improvements in the long term, or would it be exchanging one marginalized position for another?

Decisions made by senior staff in social services, without any involvement of Deaf people

The final problem mentioned, that of the ignorance of managers in making decisions which affect Deaf people's lives, is a common complaint of service users in general and is partly the product of bureaucratic hierarchies. Involving service users in planning and monitoring services has been a low-level and fragmented process to date but some authorities are now addressing this work with more vigour in readiness for the implementation of the National Health Service and Community Care Act 1990. The Deaf community is uniquely placed to take up this role and has done so in a few areas.

All of the above comments made by Deaf people lead us into major areas of significance in the role of Social Worker with Deaf People, most of which will be explored later, but first we need to set the role in its historical context and then to examine more comprehensively the position of Social Workers with Deaf People and what it is they actually do.

1 The development of social work with Deaf people

1.1 The missioners

> My wife and I lived in a flat over the Reading Centre and entered
> fully into the day-to-day life of the local deaf people, at home, at
> work and at play, in their pleasures and sorrows.
>
> (Firth, 1989)

Firth, in his book *Chosen Vessels*, about the lives of workers with Deaf
people from 1860 to 1960, captures the spirit of the life of the missioner in
his evocative tribute to the founders of welfare care of Deaf people in the
UK. This group are of seminal importance, in that they established the base
from which modern services have developed; they pioneered Deaf Centres
and Societies across the UK; they introduced the first training for Deaf
workers; and they influenced national voluntary organizations in a major
way. Lysons (1965) believes that the first centre, then known as a mission,
was opened in Edinburgh in 1818. Some 20 years later, similar centres
emerged in the large conurbations in England, often near to residential
schools.

◀ Reading
This would be a good point at which to read Article 7.1, 'The Development of Local
Voluntary Societies for Adult Deaf Persons in England' by Kenneth Lysons in Reader
Two.

You will notice in his article in Reader Two that Lysons makes the interesting point that
with the expansion of Victorian charity, whilst many other groups were becoming the
domain of philanthropists, this was less so for Deaf people, as they were less likely to
make the 'giver' feel good because of the communication barrier. Consequently, the
base of charitable concern for Deaf people was narrower than for many other groups
and tended to be drawn from:

1   Those who were Deaf themselves.
2   Families with Deaf members, particularly children of Deaf parents.
3   Those who, by chance, came into contact with Deaf people, notably employers
    and the clergy.   ◀

left to own devises
abnormal —
no progress in
standards

ITQ
What might be the effects on the Deaf community of the narrow basis of
charitable concern arising from the three groups mentioned above?

◄ Comment

Lysons suggests that this narrow base of the missions for Deaf people meant that the broader philanthropic concerns that applied to other groups, such as blind people, were missing. Those who were Deaf themselves were interested in the provision of meeting places for Deaf people. The other foci of the missions, initiated by employers and the clergy, were the encouragement of financial independence by the provision of training for employment and religious instruction. In responding to this ITQ, you may also have considered the implications of the power relationship between providers and Deaf people which is a recurring theme of this block. ◄

From the 1840s the number of missions grew, with many of the pioneers moving around the country starting new missions. Often the work was continued by the second generation, the offspring of the original missioners. By 1932 the Eichholz Report (Eichholz, 1932) identified sixty missions serving 34,000 Deaf people and as a result of this survey a Ministry of Health circular was issued, empowering local authorities to give grant aid to the missions to support their employment placement services. But what else did the missioners undertake in their work with Deaf people? Firth describes a common view of the missioner in the following extract:

> I remember being the Guest Speaker at the Annual General Meeting of the Mission at Walsall during Griffiths' term of office. I found out afterwards that Griffiths had made all the arrangements for the meeting, had sent out all the official notices and invitations, drawn up the Annual report including the Statement of Accounts (he was acting Treasurer, and always paid himself his own wages), had bought the tea and sandwiches, set up the tables and chairs, welcomed those who attended, interpreted the proceedings throughout in sign language to the Deaf people present—except for my own speech which I delivered myself, giving him a welcome break!—handed the Hon. Treasurer the Balance Sheet which the latter signed as far as I could see without even reading it; and read out the Annual Report on behalf of the Hon. Secretary—to whom this was apparently also news; ending by proposing the Vote of Thanks to all concerned, though nobody thought of returning the compliment.

(Firth, 1989)

Whilst there is undoubtedly some truth in the caricature portrayed, many missioners would be perhaps more accurately captured by another description by Firth of workers who were involved in 'visiting, advising, interpreting, job finding, organization and management'. He believed the missioners focused their work on a minority of Deaf people who were truly helped.

In 1929 the missioners established the first training course in welfare work with Deaf people, a 3-year in-service programme for those employed in Deaf Centres. Later, in 1964, the College of Deaf Welfare was established, creating a full-time course. This course ran for 5 years and was superseded by courses in general social work, followed by a post-qualifying course on deafness. This period is viewed by some as the 'golden age' of work with Deaf people, when the only college of Deaf welfare was founded.

ITQ

Why might Deaf people feel the time of the missioners was:

(a) a 'golden age'; *— past — better comms — three f Deaf an*

(b) a time of oppression? *— everything done for them*

Deaf people may have felt that the missioners gave them instant access to sources of help and their ready availability was appreciated. You may wish to reflect upon the views of the 1880 Committee (see the Introduction to this unit) in this context. However, Deaf people could also consider the missioners as a barrier to direct access to resources and information.

1.2 Local voluntary agencies

As mentioned in Section 1.1, the first statutory funding for deaf services became available in 1933 and by 1945 forty-five local voluntary societies were grant aided by their local authorities. Voluntary organizations, as not-for-profit, non-statutory agencies, may be run by unpaid volunteers, but in the Deaf field, as in other areas, those providing social work services now invariably employ professionally qualified staff. By 1962, the number of local voluntary organizations for Deaf people in England and Wales had grown to 101, out of a possible 128 local authority areas; most of these voluntary organizations had agency agreements to provide services on behalf of their local authority. In 1960, however, it had become mandatory for local authorities to provide services, either directly or through an agency agreement, by which time competing forces started to erode the concept of voluntary bases for social work. In general, local authorities were beginning to take a more direct role in providing services in areas traditionally provided by the voluntary sector (an example of this was the meals on wheels services) and it seems that, just as the voluntary societies for the Deaf had reached their zenith, the ground was being cut from beneath them. The Younghusband Report made a number of recommendations relating to Deaf services: *1959*

(a) Local authorities should take a more direct interest in the welfare of the deaf.

(b) A proportion of local authority welfare officers should learn to make adequate contact with deaf people.

(c) Where greater understanding and fluency of communication is required local authorities should either continue to use the services of voluntary organisations or employ their own trained and experienced staff for the purpose.

(d) The aim of local authority provision for the deaf should be to establish a 'high standard of service without establishing a separate service'.

(e) Local authorities should ensure that spiritual ministration is available to the deaf but should not take over this function themselves.

(f) A case-work service should be provided for deaf people who need it even if this service must initially be attempted through an interpreter.

(Younghusband Report, 1959)

This report gave the local authorities a clear lead which culminated over the next 20 years in a steady transfer of the provision of services to the state sector, so that by 1988 there were only twenty-one voluntary agents out of 109 local authorities in England and Wales (RNID, 1988). The majority of these (thirteen) were agents of county councils, whilst the minority (five) served eight metropolitan districts. It is noticeable that more voluntary agents have survived in rural areas than in the conurbations, where the societies originated.

The charismatic leaders of voluntary agencies may be a disappearing breed, but many principal officers remain nationally active in the mould of their predecessors, particularly within national voluntary organizations. They are also almost exclusively a male group, whilst the majority of basic grade workers are female, which reflects the pattern in social services departments and society in general, where few senior managers are women.

A survey carried out by the Royal National Institute for the Deaf (RNID) identified seven local authorities which fund both their own services and a voluntary agent (RNID, 1988). The majority of authorities, however, fund agents to provide the whole range of social services and many agents appear to be undertaking a wide variety of work including aspects of statutory child care. Some voluntary agencies, noticeably in Birmingham, have not taken on the statutory role themselves, but act as co-workers, consultants and interpreters for the authority staff. There is no evaluation of these various combinations of service and so it is virtually impossible to assess which ones are successful and in what circumstances. The government push towards a more mixed range of services from the state, voluntary and private sectors, combined with the need to specify service aims, is likely to draw much more attention to these issues. It is possible that local voluntary organizations for Deaf people could lead these new developments, as the voluntary sector already figures significantly in service provision.

ITQ

What are the implications of services for Deaf people being based within local voluntary organizations?

◀ Comment

Advantages

You may have thought, amongst other things, that voluntary organizations are the natural base for the Deaf community; that services based with these are in much closer contact with Deaf people, formally and informally; that there will therefore be fewer barriers to securing services; and that as they are focusing on one user group, they can design their services specifically for them. This is particularly important in terms of communication skills and it is accepted that all staff in voluntary organizations will develop skills in this area. Voluntary organizations can choose how to use their resources and so have more opportunity to innovate. The base allows a natural contact with the Deaf community, which can then be used as a resource, and the expansion of community- and group-work approaches sits easily in a voluntary setting.

Disadvantages

You may feel that to place social work with a range of services in the voluntary sector at one base perpetrates a restricted access point for Deaf people, replicating the single gatekeeper model which makes access to many services dependent upon contact with a social worker. Working with small communities heightens difficulties of confidentiality and can increase role confusion. Links with peer professionals may be weaker and knowledge of general resources available in social services may be more limited. A poor voluntary agency can maintain the dependency culture and disguise the gaps in services from the appropriate authorities. The role of voluntary organizations in the provision of services for Deaf people is discussed further in Section 5. ◄

1.3 A rare species or dying breed?

Information on the characteristics of Social Workers with Deaf People is sparse, but in 1977 the Advisory Committee on Services for Hearing Impaired[1] People (ACSHIP) identified 379 posts in 109 English and Welsh local authorities (DHSS, 1977). More than half of those posts were located in voluntary agencies which provided services on behalf of their local authority. Over the next decade the number of posts reduced marginally and by 1988 only a quarter were still based in voluntary agencies. It may be assumed that, because more workers were based in local authorities, services would be integrated and the workers would be similar to their generic colleagues. In fact, although the population of workers with Deaf people with a generic social work qualification had risen, they still lagged behind their generic colleagues; 69 per cent of Social Workers with Deaf People are qualified in social work compared to 85 per cent of generic social workers. ACSHIP recommended that for a minimum level of service, each authority should have at least one dually qualified worker; that is, qualified in basic social work and in the specialism. In 1988 only 17 per cent of authorities in England had achieved this target and only 30 per cent had the level of sign language skills recommended in the *Say It Again* Report; that is, CACDP[2] or SASLI[3] Stage II. As this level of communication is viewed as an absolute minimum for practice, the picture emerges of a small group of workers, lagging behind their generic colleagues, who did not even have the recommended minimum levels of training within their chosen specialism. It may not, therefore, be too surprising that recruitment into the specialism is poor; in 1988 fourteen authorities had no service at all and 52 per cent of posts advertised between 1984 and 1988 were either filled with unqualified people or not filled at all (Peckford and Hawcroft, 1990).

A number of interacting factors have contributed to the above picture, including the lack of management interest in most authorities which existed until comparatively recently, lack of salary incentives, lack of acknowledgement of the time required to train for essential skills and lack

---

[1] In this section the term 'hearing impaired' is sometimes used, whereas in the rest of the unit it is not. This reflects the form of some job descriptions and advertisements which use the term.

[2] Council for the Advancement of Communication with Deaf People.

[3] Scottish Association of Sign Language Interpreters.

of promotional opportunities, all of which have been highlighted as disincentives to entering this area of work. A further disincentive has been the absence of any training in the specialism, either on basic social work courses or on post-qualifying courses. Neglect by service managers is a major contributing factor and in the government report *Say It Again*, the importance of effective management is illustrated by the fact that twenty-two out of twenty-eight recommendations relate to management issues. This report, the follow-up work by the Social Services Inspectorate, and the impetus generated by the Disabled Persons Act have all culminated in senior management in social services departments starting to address the issues. As they do so, some have been surprised by the size and complexity of these, which they had formerly believed to be narrow. Once deafness is on the agenda of agencies, specialist workers and national and local voluntary organizations, together with Deaf people, need to grasp the opportunity to exert some influence.

1.4 What do they do?

The following is an actual job description, which outlines the many tasks to be undertaken in a local authority by a Social Worker with Deaf People. You may be surprised at the broad range of duties specified:

Department: Social Services

Job Designation: Social Worker for the Deaf

Post Objectives: To provide a specialist service for the deaf and hard of hearing

Duties	Tasks
1 The provision of a specialist casework service to the deaf and hard of hearing and their families	1.1 To make initial visits to all those referred to the Department for help or advice
	1.2 To visit or contact periodically all clients on the register
	1.3 To provide specialist advice/follow-up as required
	1.4 To provide a comprehensive social casework service to deaf people and their families either directly or through other workers
	1.5 To work with groups and participate
	1.6 To act as interpreter
	1.7 To keep records and make such reports as may be necessary
	1.8 To make recommendations for adaptations or aids under the provision of the Chronically Sick and Disabled Persons Act, and advise on the use of such equipment
	1.9 To provide advice to Social Workers and residential staff who are working with the deaf, and to take part in training programmes or seminars
	1.10 Liaison with voluntary or statutory agencies, and the establishment of effective communication links with the Department
	1.11 To publicize available services
2 Identification of need	2.1 Discussion with other specialist workers, deaf people and their families
	2.2 Participation in Surveys
3 Assist in developing a comprehensive social service for the deaf in the area	3.1 To initiate or participate in such projects as may be agreed

This fairly typical job description for a Social Worker with Deaf People is from an authority which at that time had one worker (quoted in *A Secret Service*, Department of Health, 1989). There appears to be no prioritizing of work tasks, yet it is clearly not possible for a single worker to undertake all the tasks effectively. If this job description only referred to Deaf people it would be daunting enough, but the inclusion of all hearing-impaired groups makes it impossible. Social services do have to find ways of providing services to all hearing-impaired people and they have been singularly unsuccessful in developing services to deafened and hard of hearing people. The reasons for this are partly linked to the origins of the service, which in the voluntary sector focused on BSL users and this focus was adopted by social services without close examination. Once inside the statutory sector, authorities were slow to recognize the distinct groups of hearing-impaired people. Cleveland authority, which has one of the largest social work teams in the country, listed the following nine groups as service users:

Pre-lingually deaf people

Post-lingually deaf people

Mentally ill and deaf people

Deaf and blind people

Deafened people

Additionally handicapped (*sic*) and deaf people

Deaf people from ethnic minority groups

Deaf people in adult life

Older deaf people

(Keogan, 1986)

This list is not exhaustive but gives an indication of the breadth of demand likely to face social services, which in the main have failed to organize services to meet this demand. The response of departments to the largest group, older people with hearing loss, which outnumbers all the others, has been at best inadequate, at worst scandalous. Many departments make the assumption that this group will be adequately dealt with by general provision for older people, but this is rarely the case. A group of common characteristics underpins the sparse provision of services to all hearing-impaired groups in that the services are under-resourced in posts and budgets, they are reactive and they are often inaccurately targeted.

In the job description, the two tasks which consume the greatest amount of time and resources—1.6, to act as an interpreter, and 1.8, to make recommendations for adaptations or aids under the provision of the Chronically Sick and Disabled Persons Act, and to advise on the use of such equipment—are not seen as social work tasks in other settings. Interpreting is a major plank in the provision of services to Deaf people and is given high priority by Deaf people themselves, and will be dealt with separately in Section 2.

The provision of aids to daily living is an important service both in terms of the quality of life for the service user and in terms of the high demand, which requires firm management systems. Such aids have been acknowledged as important in a number of Acts of Parliament, beginning with the National Assistance Act 1948, which opened the door to the provision of aids, through to the Chronically Sick and Disabled Persons Act

1970, which was more pro-active, and the Disabled Persons Act 1986, which reaffirms the right to have appropriate equipment (see the *Legislation Booklet* for further details of these Acts). In relation to aids to daily living, none of this legislation refers especially to Deaf people but to people with disabilities in general. Some Deaf people feel strongly that they should not have to be categorized as disabled in order to receive equipment they require to live life to the full. In fact, they do not have to register with the social services department to receive services, but as they would be dealt with under the same legislation it amounts to nearly the same thing. It is perhaps surprising that Deaf people have not chosen to refuse to register in greater numbers.

ITQ

What reasons might Deaf people give as to why they should or should not be registered as disabled?

◀ Comment

A parallel could be drawn with spectacles, or dental treatment, in that one does not have to register as disabled to receive spectacles or a dental plate which are aids to living. As you will appreciate, the discussion as to whether Deaf people are disabled or not is a recurring theme of this course. ◀

Although the number of Deaf people, as opposed to hearing-impaired people, in any local authority area is small, they are usually identified and it is lamentable that authorities have not been more pro-active in promoting technological aids to independence. The cost of such aids is low and in most cases individual items will be between £30 and £200 (at the time of writing in 1990)—for the equipment currently available it would probably cost less than £1,000 per head to provide a comprehensive range. This figure is negligible compared to money spent on other items of equipment but authorities have not sought out Deaf people and offered them the full range available. Not only is this deplorable, it is also short-sighted as many of these aids will reduce reliance on social work staff. The clearest example of this is the text telephone, which allows Deaf people, for the first time, to have access to the telephone network to make private calls. Increasingly, public institutions, such as the emergency services, British Airways and the Samaritans, are installing this technology. In a *Community Care* article (April, 1990), a group of Deaf service users attested to the 'phenomenal difference to lifestyles' that technical aids had brought them, but also described the obstacles erected by local authorities. One member of the group, in outlining the difficulties of obtaining simple low-cost equipment, wondered: 'Why do we always have to give good reasons for wanting to contact each other? We are just like everyone else. People who can hear don't have to ask permission to do such everyday things' (King, 1990).

Despite the impetus created by the Disabled Persons Act, such comments from Deaf service users make the process of service provision sound more like a reflection of the Poor Law, with its attitude towards the 'deserving' and 'undeserving', than a rights-based service as intended by the 1986 Act.

Deaf lumped tog with disabled.

This may be partly because the Deaf element of services has only started to be examined relatively recently and so retains outmoded attitudes, but it is probably also part of the response to disability in general, which is reactive, rather than pro-active, and is also low status. The picture is further complicated by the inclusion of all disabled groups as one entity and so details about assessment criteria, budgets and work-load management are hidden, making sensible management decisions impossible.

A research report by the RNID *So Little for So Many* (RNID, 1987) confirmed all the above confusions, showing that most authorities could not say how many pieces of equipment they had provided, nor how much had been spent. The report suggests that difficulties of recruiting suitable staff were probably a greater inhibitor of service development than budget restrictions. Authorities are unlikely to be able to untangle this mess without a determined recruitment drive and a vigorous application of financial control.

ITQ

Can you think of a system, which Deaf people might prefer, from which they could obtain the equipment they require? Try to list some alternatives.

A number of groups of disabled people have put forward alternative systems, including the following:

1   Pay all disabled people a personal allowance, with which they can choose to purchase equipment.
2   Fund resource centres, managed and staffed by people with disabilities, where aids can be displayed and advice given. The Derbyshire Centre for Independent Living is pioneering this approach.

It seems unlikely that there is the political will in the present climate to reorganize radically the basis for meeting the rights of disabled people to have the equipment necessary to lead independent lives.

◀ Activity 2

Contact your local social services department and ask about their services for Deaf people. Make a few notes for yourself on these. ◀

1.5 Real social work?

Debates about the nature of social work with Deaf people have existed for many years, usually concentrating around such basic questions as:

Δ   Is it real social work and is it, therefore, similar to other forms of social work?

Δ   Is it a specialism and is it necessary to have specialist workers?

1.5.1 Is it real social work?

One definition of social work has already been given in the Introduction. A related conception comes from the Barclay Report *Social Workers: Their Roles and Their Tasks* (Barclay, 1982). The Barclay Committee received 350 representations and from these they identified two major components of social work. These were (i) counselling and (ii) social care planning, both of which could be performed in a variety of settings and with a variety of service users. For example, a social worker in a hospital supporting a dying patient, and one in a family centre working to reunite a child with its parents, may, at first glance, appear to be doing very different tasks, but may be using the same techniques. Defining social work has often been confused by the many contexts in which it can be practised and by the concentration on the individuality of users rather than on common strands. All of this may be further complicated by social work being practised in multi-function agencies. Very few organizations in the UK provide social work exclusively and state agencies, particularly social services departments, provide many other services, ranging from meals on wheels, to burials for those unable to afford private funerals.

In addition to the two major components of social work mentioned above, the Barclay Report suggests further tasks which are essential to social work. These include assessment, advice giving, provision of practical services, and acting as an intermediary. All of these are major features of the day-to-day work of Social Workers with Deaf People. As there are no comparative studies, it is impossible to calculate whether the emphasis and the time spent on individual tasks is different for Social Workers with Deaf People compared to other social workers. It is, of course, entirely likely that there would be marked differences between social workers in different settings, irrespective of the user group. Much of the work of Social Workers with Deaf People involves counselling and organizing social care, whether it be arranging support services to help an older person in the community, or obtaining a day nursery placement for a child.

It is difficult to compare the work of Social Workers with Deaf People with that of other social workers because of the range of other tasks Social Workers with Deaf People undertake. Consider the two examples of cases reported below, both based on actual cases. Although the cases are similar in many respects, to what extent do you feel extra demands are made upon the Social Worker with Deaf People, or extra skills expected?

> **Social worker:**
> Mary was a rather dull, very anxious girl who had spent much of her childhood at special boarding schools. Her parents had high expectations and were deeply disappointed in their daughter. From about the age of 16 she behaved in a rather promiscuous way, having two pregnancies and abortions. She then became pregnant again by a West Indian man whom she hoped would support her …
>
> … Her determination to keep the child and bring it up herself was unshakeable, even though the father was clearly not in fact offering any support or relationship. The social worker arranged a mother and baby home and James was born uneventfully. From the outset it was clear to those around her that Mary was finding it extremely hard to manage the ordinary practicalities of looking after a baby, and this was

made more difficult by her own very high standards set for herself and for the baby. Mary's parents continued to refuse to support her. ...

... She became quite depressed, largely through her isolation. ...

... As James grew older, Mary found it increasingly difficult to manage him. He responded to her inconsistency by becoming very aggressive both at home and in the nursery.

(Barclay, 1982)

Social Worker with Deaf People:
Rose was profoundly deaf from birth, the only deaf person in her family, and had attended a local residential school. She left school without academic qualifications, was under confident, unable to adequately communicate with her parents, but proficient in BSL. At nineteen she became pregnant and lived with a hearing man, who promised to marry her. By the time the baby was born he had left and Rose needed emotional and practical support from the social worker to manage her baby. On attending nursery, the little girl was said to be noisy, attention seeking and aggressive. Rose set high standards for herself and was determined to manage her own life, despite periods of intense isolation when the baby was small.

(Author's own social work practice)

ITQ
In the light of your thoughts on the above case histories, and in preparation for the next section, what might be the arguments for social work with Deaf people being carried out by:

(a) specialist Social Workers with Deaf People;   — understand Deaf way

or

(b) generic social workers with specialist interpreters?   — same as anyone else

---

◀ Comment
This debate is not confined to work with Deaf people. You may find it useful to make comparisons with work with ethnic minority groups. ◀

1.5.2 Is it a specialism?

Greater emphasis has been placed on this issue than on any other in discussions about social work with Deaf people. Communication is often viewed as all important and, whilst it is clearly impossible to undertake effective social work without meaningful communication, such communication is not as simple as it seems.

Stevenson (1981) defines areas of specialization in social work as: (a) setting; (b) method of work; and (c) client groups. She suggests that (b) has not been a major focus in the UK and that in (a) the distinctive nature lies in the agency context. Work with Deaf people has mostly been described as a specialism in relation to (c). Stevenson maintains that specialist knowledge in one area allows expertise to build up and that when any of us are in

Specialisation
social work =
i) setting
ii) method of work
iii) client group

Deaf = iii

23

difficulty we would prefer to consult those who have expertise that we do not possess ourselves. The range of tasks within social work is very broad and has to be divided in one way or another. Some commentators believe that division into specialist user groups is an efficient way to deliver appropriate services. On these grounds, social work with Deaf people would seem to qualify as a specialist area.

The discussions created by the separation of interpreting from social work have led some people to suggest that social work services should be provided by a social worker with an interpreter. The difficulty of conducting intensive interviews through a third party has been mentioned in Unit 6 with respect to mental health services, but this, together with Deaf people's strong preference for workers with a knowledge and understanding of Deaf culture, points to the need for some specialists. Social work methods, which involve much reliance on verbal interaction, may need to be modified to be usable with Deaf people. The presence of an interpreter would only allow the non-specialist to use his or her usual range of techniques: specialists should be modifying methods to suit Deaf people, and even developing new approaches.

Social Workers with Deaf People have wrestled with the dilemma of, on the one hand, needing to build trust and contact with the Deaf community to enable them to perform their role effectively and, on the other hand, keeping sufficient distance to be able to act impartially and with authority when necessary. Particularly when dealing with statutory areas of social work, such as taking children into care, social workers need a thorough understanding of the cultural and social effects of deafness, balanced by a clear view of their role as an agent of the state in protecting children. Deaf parents have been confused by social workers exercising these powers, because they have been surprised that workers for Deaf people can act against their wishes. This raises the question of whether it is possible to operate as a social worker in any meaningful way if the powers and responsibilities of that role are not made explicit.

2 Interpreting

You were introduced to discussion on interpreting in Unit 3, and in Video Two you were able to see interpreting in action. The interpreting you saw in that video, and which you might have seen on television programmes, is only one area of interpreting—that of platform interpreting. Interpreters work in a range of areas—for example, at Open University D251 course team meetings and in classrooms. Social workers, when they undertake an interpreting role, would usually interpret for one Deaf person and often in interviews with public officials. Whether this should be part of the remit for social workers is discussed in this section.

2.1 The role of the interpreter

A Deaf man appears in Court for a motoring offence. The interpreter is the local Social Worker with Deaf People. During the court proceedings the Deaf man swears at the magistrate in sign language, but it is not interpreted, so the magistrate is unaware of this.

ITQ

Why do you think the interpreter did not convey the swearing to the magistrate? Was this correct?   Yes

---

Amongst the reasons you may have considered could be embarrassment, over-protection, lack of understanding, politeness. In fact, the interpreter, who was both a social worker *and* a registered interpreter, judged that the Deaf man was unaware that swearing in court was unacceptable and that it could have led to further charges being made against him. Leaving aside the question of how many members of the public would know this, do you feel it was a legitimate reason to modify the Deaf person's response? This example was taken from the author's personal experience and in discussing it with Deaf people an interesting point was put forward: it was suggested that sometimes a Deaf person will use a sign in different ways, so that whilst it may be used as swearing in one instance, it may have a slightly different and broader meaning on other occasions. How does an interpreter know this, especially in a formal setting, such as a court, where it is difficult to double-check meanings? This perhaps demonstrates that sign language, just like other languages, is operating within a certain cultural context.

If you suggested, in answer to the ITQ, that an interpreter should have conveyed the full content and intent of the message, this is a reasonable view, if the Deaf man had been fully aware of this also. However, he may have expected the interpreter to act in a 'helping' role, thereby protecting him from his own actions. This expectation may be related to the social work role which may legitimately include advising and guiding. This example clearly illustrates the tension between combining the roles of interpreting and social work and raises the question of whether it is possible to have good practice in either area when the roles are combined.

◀ Reading
Now turn to Reader Two, to look at Article 7.4, 'Sign Language Interpreting: An Emerging Profession' by Liz Scott-Gibson. ◀

Having read Scott-Gibson's article, would you now revise your earlier answers to the questions about the interpreter in court? Scott-Gibson traces the slow and sometimes painful process of separation of the symbiotic relationship which has developed between social work and interpreting in the UK. As indicated in Section 1, the former role was first invested in the early missioners and combined with their other roles of advising and helping Deaf people with many areas of their lives. The state-employed social workers inherited this multiplicity of roles, which was further complicated by their dual responsibilities of care and control. This has now squeezed social workers into a most uncomfortable position and whilst many would agree with the need to separate the two functions, social workers are reluctant to withdraw their interpreting services in the absence of alternative provision.

ITQ

If you had to arrange for the Deaf man mentioned earlier to attend court, with an interpreter, how would you try to do this? — SW t Deaf
Reg Interpret

A logical place to start would be the court itself, but many court officials would have no idea how to obtain an interpreter direct and most would rely on the police and possibly the probation service to find one for them. In some areas, particularly urban ones, the police will have a list of interpreters, including sign language users. If, after numerous telephone calls to some or all of the above, you were eventually given the names of interpreters, your task would not be ended. Any list of interpreters is likely to comprise local social workers and/or freelance interpreters. We have already touched on the difficulties of combining a professional interpreting role with social work and this becomes much more problematic in legal settings. Courts view social workers as local authority staff whose role is to provide background information in reports to assist the courts in making decisions. In view of this, they will ask for advice and opinions from the social worker and this role is incompatible with acting as an interpreter at the same time. It is not unusual for magistrates and judges to expect workers to step from one role to the other and they may not be aware of the conflict this gives rise to. For many years social workers have battled with the ignorance of the courts and even when they say quite clearly that an independent interpreter must be engaged, so that they themselves are able to undertake the social work task, they have often met with resistance from court officials, the police and even their own managers. An example of how the rights of Deaf people can be infringed by well-meaning officials, is highlighted in the case of care proceedings.

> *A social service department is taking care proceedings against a Deaf couple, to try to remove their children from them. The parents are well known to the Social Worker with Deaf People, who has been involved in collecting evidence to support the department's case.*

It is inconceivable that the social worker could act as an interpreter in this type of situation, as the social worker is the department's agent and there would be a clear conflict of interest. Unfortunately, many of the professionals involved have been unaware of the issues and it is not too many years ago that the social worker would have been placed in a most invidious position. Even today, it is most likely to be the social worker who will point out the difficulties and it will often quite unfairly be left to them to find an independent interpreter. You may be starting to realize that these issues are far more complex than they first appear and that if the social worker does not alert the system to the possible infringement of Deaf people's rights, there may not be anybody else who will do so.

If you were in one of the few areas of the country where freelance interpreters were well established and known to the relevant court officials, you may well still have some difficulties. As you read in the Reader article by Liz Scott-Gibson, there are only ninety-one registered interpreters in the UK and many of these are unavailable on a daily basis; it is clear, therefore, that courts will be using people who are not registered. This then leaves them with the problem of knowing whether the person is both competent to act as an interpreter and experienced in legal settings. As the courts do not know which questions to ask in order to establish this, and as there are insufficient registered interpreters available, the risk of interpreting services being poor is high and it will be a game of fortune for Deaf people for some time to come.

However, the recent emergence of local authority based interpreter units may go some way to solving some of these problems. There are currently only two such units, based in Nottingham and Manchester, and as models of service they have broken the previous mould of the exclusive social work service and other areas look set to follow. Such units are managed outside of social work line management and so can act independently if required. This solves some of the problems mentioned above in relation to the court setting and similar issues applying in other contexts.

A very different area of work to that of court work, but which equally requires independent interpreters, is in consultation exercises with Deaf service users. It would be unfair on both service users and social workers if the latter were asked to interpret when the quality of their own services was being discussed. The two interpreter units presently offer no more than a handful of interpreters, which is a drop in the ocean, but if the model is replicated they may then become central points, providing not only interpreter services but also advice on all matters relating to interpreting issues. They could, for instance, assist community agencies to obtain an appropriate interpreter, at a fair fee; and they could help Deaf people to be involved in monitoring quality of service and in using complaints systems when necessary.

Whilst the chances of locating an interpreter with the necessary skills and experience are still quite slim in many areas of the country, there are some signs that the emerging profession, as outlined by Scott-Gibson, is establishing itself. The pioneering work of the Council for Advancement of Communication with Deaf People has been described in Reader Two and now that its focus is as an examining body, it is in the business of setting standards. The groundswell of courses at the lowest communication levels— for example, just under 8,000 candidates passed Stage I of the Council's certificate in the period 1987–90—is a marvellous public relations exercise. In many areas the general public are demanding sign language classes and if these classes are taught by Deaf people they are a vehicle for the positive contribution of Deaf people and their community to society at large. On their own these basic courses, mostly taught in night-school weekly classes, will not produce many individuals able to take up work at the interpreting level. However, the availability of paid work, particularly in communication support to employment training, has opened a channel for training and employment, and the communicators courses also mentioned in the Reader have been a fertile bed for producing communicators.

Further evidence of the professionalization of interpreting is the establishment of professional organizations of interpreters in England and Scotland[4] and the recent move by the major national voluntary organizations to set standard fees. The shortage of available interpreters has led to wild variations in fees charged, which has confused and, in some instances, incensed agencies needing to engage interpreters and so the move to recommend standard levels at least gives some national guidelines. The setting up of a Committee of Enquiry by the Department of Health to investigate interpreting is also a welcome initiative in further promoting the status of the profession.

The value of interpreters to both hearing and Deaf people has become publicly recognized, but both hearing and Deaf people need to understand how to use an interpreter. The hearing recipient needs to be aware that he or she cannot expect answers from the interpreter whilst interpreting is taking place, that seating and lighting are important, and that these are only some of the issues to be considered. Likewise, Deaf people may need to think about how they use an interpreter—for example, whether, when entering a doctor's surgery, the Deaf patient or the interpreter enters first.

◀ Activity 3

Imagine you are the interpreter referred to above and then list the consequences of:

(a) you entering the room first; ~ *dominant – think polite*

(b) the Deaf person being first to enter. ◀ *– greeted by Dr. Lool? more positive*

2.2 Establishing standards of interpreting

Many Deaf people will still be working within the framework in which the interpreter is there to 'help', so that they feel powerless as the ones being 'helped'. In a paper to the European Sign Language Interpreters Conference in 1988, Terry Riley said: 'the developments are outstripping the consumers' awareness of the services' (Riley, 1988).

Certainly, anecdotes are told in which some Deaf people say that they cannot use the independent interpreters on offer because it would make the social worker, whom they have known for 20 years, feel unwanted! Of course, new interpreters will have to build up trust with Deaf people which will take some time. Asked how he recognizes a good interpreter, Billy Lambert, a Deaf man working for the RNID as a Regional Officer, in conversation with the unit author, suggested:

> 1 The interpreter is well prepared, has time to meet the Deaf person before any assignment (if unknown to them) and arrives in good time.
>
> 2 They should be dressed appropriately, not too bright colours and not too much jewellery.

---

[4] The Association of Sign Language Interpreters (ASLI) in England and the Scottish Association of Sign Language Interpreters (SASLI) in Scotland.

3 The interpreter should have the confidence to stop proceedings if not understanding.

4 They appear to the Deaf person to be competent in English and BSL.

5 They have a good expressive vocal range.

6 They do not interject with their own point of view.

7 The interpreter should afford respect to the Deaf person.

(Transcript of a conversation in BSL)

Some of the above points are easy for a Deaf person to judge—dress and timekeeping, for example—but others, such as points 4 and 5, are less easy. It may be possible for some evaluation of the expressive signing of the interpreters to be made by matching this to the hearing person's style and speed and so on. However, it is much more difficult for the Deaf person to know if their own signing is being faithfully interpreted. The same Deaf man says he was shocked when, following a lecture he gave, the interpretation which had been tape recorded was typed for him. Until that time he had not been aware that the interpretation could be inaccurate, stilted and not in standard English. In recent years, Deaf people have been more aware of this aspect of interpreting, as more of them have moved into professional posts requiring public speaking and chairing of meetings. In such settings, Terry Riley's suggestion that an interpreter is 'one who sets me free' would mean that Deaf people could get on with the job in hand and not have to worry about misunderstandings.

What happens, though, if a Deaf person is very unhappy with the performance of an interpreter? Very often this will result in that particular interpreter not being used by that Deaf person again, but this does not help the interpreter to improve. The Deaf person could complain directly to the interpreter, or to the organizer of the event (if appropriate), or to the interpreter's employer (if he or she has one). All registered interpreters are bound by a code of practice, which includes informing Deaf people of the complaints procedure. As consumerism invades the caring services, perhaps more systems will be designed in consultation with Deaf people and information will be automatically available, including on video, to inform Deaf people of their rights.

2.3 Interpreting in a social work setting

◄ Reading
Turn to Reader Two and look at Article 7.5, 'Social Work and Interpreting' by David Moorhead. ◄

Moorhead suggests that the continued use of social workers as interpreters will prolong practices which effectively deny Deaf people control over their own lives. This is a view which has been accepted by many, including social workers, in recent years. However, it has proved difficult for social workers to withdraw in the absence of alternative provision.

What might be the advantages and disadvantages to Deaf people if:

(a) social workers fulfil the interpreting role; — *Know Deaf person –*

(b) they withdraw from interpreting. — *independant SW + Deaf prop*

Interpreting has never sat easily within social services departments, probably because of the conflict between the agencies' care and control function and the independent model of interpreting as discussed by Moorhead in the Reader article. It is also part of service provision, largely by default, in that it may be mentioned in legislation and reports, but it has been largely misunderstood by the managers within social services departments. As they become more enlightened about the relevant issues, they may insist that social work staff do not use their time on interpreting. Whilst the concern expressed by Scott-Gibson in her Reader article, about some employers viewing interpreting as part of the social work task, is valid, this should not mask the need for interpreting in social services. Just as any other agency should make its services accessible, so should social services and, with the current scarcity of front-line staff training in sign language skills, this is likely to be via an interpreter. This may be for a simple enquiry dealt with by a receptionist, or duty officer, or for a home care or occupational therapy assessment—such tasks are not carried out by social workers, but they are provided by social services departments and may be needed by Deaf people. They should therefore be made available to them in their first language.

There are also some occasions when Social Workers with Deaf People require independent interpreters in highly complex social work situations. Such situations could include assessments under the Mental Health Act for compulsory admission or investigation of child abuse. Ideally, an interpreter outside of the department should be used, but because of the current low numbers of these interpreters, and lack of training in social work contexts, they may well be unsuitable. In the thrust forward to separate interpreting from social work, the positive elements from this relationship should not be thrown away. If Social Workers with Deaf People have previously acted as interpreters, then they surely ought to know how to make appropriate use of specialist interpreters within their department. Also, as the agency has gained some awareness, then why not capitalize on this and have an in-house interpreter to do social services interpreting where required? The role of an in-house interpreter could be broadened to include training so that all staff could be taught how to make best use of an interpreter and how to improve their own general communication skills.

All other areas of interpreting for outside agencies in the future should be referred by social services departments to units or freelance interpreters. Until there are more developed systems in place, social services departments could usefully work with Deaf people to monitor the quality of freelance provision. Unless the other agencies, particularly health agencies, are made aware of the need to provide interpreters, social services only mask the true demand and delay the time when the appropriate agency will take responsibility.

I will end this section by looking at just three of the points out of the twelve contained in the Code of Practice for registered interpreters, which is obligatory. Imagine the position of a social worker, who is also a registered interpreter, in relation to these points:

> Code of Practice no. 3. An interpreter shall not function in any situation where his/her impartiality could be seriously questioned.
>
> (CACDP, 1985)

As an agent of his or her employer, the social worker could not act impartially in any situation where the power of the authority is being exercised over a Deaf person. These powers are wide ranging and include the compulsory admission of children and adults to residential care, and the power to inspect premises. To protect Deaf people's rights and to adhere to the Code of Practice, the social worker could not interpret in any such situations.

> Code of Practice no. 6. Interpreters shall always keep all matters confidential that they have access to, whilst acting as an interpreter.
>
> (Ibid.)

Social workers are bound by their department's procedures, which would not sanction silence if they became aware of child abuse, or somebody who was dangerous, and so the two procedures are contradictory. How could the social worker behave ethically in this situation? Even in less vivid examples, it is often difficult to remember which information they have gained as social workers, and which as interpreters, and whilst high degrees of confidentiality are expected in both areas, it is not always possible to keep the two distinct.

> Code of Practice no. 7. Interpreters must not counsel, advise, influence or offer personal opinions.
>
> (Ibid.)

On many occasions in the past, social workers would act both as interpreters and as social workers in the same interview, and it is clearly totally confusing for them to counsel and advise one minute and then to interpret the next. It is obviously impossible to do justice to either role. However, it can be argued that, despite the need for separation and greater clarity between the two roles, there are some social work situations in which it is legitimate for social workers to interpret. For example, the specialist knowledge of Social Workers with Deaf People may be essential in interpreting in disclosure work in child abuse cases, or some mental health work such as interviews between Deaf people and psychiatrists. However, the roles must be kept distinct.

3 The role of Deaf people

3.1 Deaf not disabled

You will remember that, in the Introduction to this unit, it was noted that the 1880 Group had raised the issue of the conceptualization of Deaf people as a 'problem' (i.e. in effect as being 'disabled'), and that this was not acceptable to them. This issue has already been addressed and will be examined again in some depth in Unit 9, where an alternative conception, that of Deaf people forming a language minority group, will be presented. As deafness has been placed within disability in all social policy, one has to look at the general disability field when trying to trace the origins of this conception.

◀ Reading
You should now read Article 7.6, ' "We" Are Not Disabled, "You" Are' by Vic Finkelstein and Article 7.7, 'Deaf People and Minority Groups in the UK' by Jim Kyle in Reader Two and consider whether you feel Deaf people are disabled or whether they are more like people from ethnic minorities. You should make notes supporting each of these ways of categorizing Deaf people from the perspective of providing local services for them. ◀

In his booklet, *On Our Own Behalf*, Pagel (1988) points out that the first official recognition of the impact of disability on people's lives by the state was the Royal Commission on the Blind and Deaf, 1886. The only action following the Commission's Report was in the field of education and so, to counter this, the first campaigning organizations were born, controlled by disabled people. These were the National League of the Blind and what is now The British Deaf Association, both established in 1890. In both the UK and the USA the first legislation involving the state in overcoming disadvantage faced by disabled people was secured by blind people. In the UK, there was no actual statutory definition of a disabled person until the 1944 Disabled Person's (Employment) Act, closely followed by the National Assistance Act 1948. Pagel suggests that the legislation imposed new levels of medical definitions of disability with ineffective action as recommendations were empowering rather than mandatory. Disabled people formed their own organizations to counter this approach and, led by activists in the civil rights movement in the USA, founded a world-wide disability movement.

Organizations of Deaf people have been part of this movement for self-advocacy, but whilst in some areas they have taken part in the general disability movement, in many others it appears this has not happened. This may be linked to the views expressed by the 1880 Group and challenged by Vic Finkelstein in his article in Reader Two. If we accept the view of the 1880 Group and try to imagine legislation and services for Deaf people outside of the disability area, what would be the underpinning principles and the implications of these for service delivery?

What needed if Deaf not to be seen as disabled

Principle	Services
BSL accepted as a language	All state agencies provide services in BSL directly or via interpreters
	Personal communication allowance
Access through technology	All agencies provide hardware, text-telephones, computers
	Personal technology allowance via tax system
	Information on video and computers
Deaf people as providers	Employ Deaf staff
	Deaf people as foster and adoptive parents
	Deaf people as advocates
	Deaf people as information officers
All front-line staff have basic understanding of deafness	Deaf trainers provide awareness training to all agencies
Access to Deaf culture as a right	Stimulation of Deaf club network by funding and explicit promotion of the value of the culture
Deaf people with social problems require equity with others in a similar position	Social work problems dealt with by Social Workers with Deaf People who are themselves Deaf and who are qualified

3.2 How can Deaf people influence services?

The move towards consumerism has also touched social services provision, underpinned by the principle of user involvement in the Disabled Persons Act 1986. This has stimulated a number of departments to seek the views of Deaf people, though often there have been serious difficulties encountered in this process.

◀ Activity 4
What could departments do to obtain the views of Deaf people about their services? Make a list of all the things you can think of. ◀

◀ Comment
The list you made may have included the following:

Δ   Send out questionnaires etc. on individual aspects of service.

Δ   Carry out independent interviews of sample of service users—this could be done, for example, by a university research department.

Δ   Advertise the complaints procedure.

△ Publicize the right to complain and to have access to files.

△ Produce accessible publicity about services, both statutory and voluntary (now a requirement under Section 9 of the Disabled Persons Act)—use of videos in BSL should be included.

△ Arrange public meetings.

△ Ask opinions of local and national voluntary organizations.

△ Appoint Deaf representatives to committees (now a requirement under Section 10 of the Disabled Persons Act).

△ Ask front-line staff.

△ Enable Deaf people to be partners with service providers; for example, as foster parents, or by the handing over of resources to Deaf people.

△ Employ Deaf people.

All of the above require accessibility via human facilitation, as in the case of interpreters, lipspeakers and notetakers. ◄

3.3 Deaf social workers

Since the ascendency of the hearing missioners over the Deaf pioneers who started Deaf clubs, hearing professionals have been the norm. Of all the professional groups, Social Workers with Deaf People can probably claim to have more deaf members than other professional groups. However, few of these are Deaf and although there are no available statistics, the number of Deaf Social Workers with Deaf People is small. The main reason for this is the barrier created by qualifying training, which does little to facilitate Deaf students and reflects a negative attitude towards Deaf people. Those few Deaf social workers who have managed to break through the system have done so on an individual basis, often having to find their own interpreters and other support systems. The achievement of the professional qualification has often been at great cost, both financially and emotionally, to the individual who has survived, in spite of, rather than because of, the educational system.

This situation may improve if the opportunities offered by some recent developments are seized. These include those universities and polytechnics which house full-time social work courses and which are just starting to feel the impact of their equal opportunity policies. They should be finding ways to provide necessary support to students, and this is clearly being tackled in some places. This non-discriminatory approach is being encouraged by the Central Council for Education and Training in Social Work which is emphasizing the importance of such ideals in its new form of social work training. The recent announcement that students' special needs allowances are to be substantially increased, will allow the increased purchase of interpreters and other support services.

Those social workers who are Deaf seem not to have taken a political stance in relation to their work and there is no evidence that they have worked together to effect change. Is this explained by assimilation? Interestingly, Black social workers can claim some success in raising the profile of Black issues in social work. Brien (1981) in discussing this point in relation to deaf teachers of the deaf, feels that those who, after a great struggle, enter professional ranks, do little to change things. He suggests that this is because, in order to become part of the professional group, deaf people have had to accept group pressures to conform. Not all would agree with this assertion, and today, with the recognition of the importance of sign language in education and the growth of organizations such as LASER (the Language of Sign as an Educational Resource), the impact of deaf teachers is becoming more significant.

Little is known of the effect on Deaf social workers when they become professional workers in their own communities. It would be interesting to see whether research into this question would find that they are more easily accepted by service users or if there is resentment at their new role. How do Deaf people feel, for example, if statutory powers are exercised by one of their 'own' group? Do they feel betrayed, or has the professional role distanced the worker from the group? These are fascinating aspects of work with Deaf people that have received scant attention. Parallels with social work with other minority groups, particularly work with ethnic minorities, would also lead to interesting comparisons and allow us to know more about the Deaf scene by discovering the similarities and differences between the different minority groups. This is a theme which will be further explored in Unit 9.

We also know little about service users' wishes and whether they would prefer Deaf social workers for some tasks, but we do know that they have little choice at the moment. Would it help if they insisted on Deaf workers and if they lobbied employers to employ Deaf staff? Sources of information are so lacking that we do not even know whether there are some parts of social work that would be difficult for Deaf workers. Starting to collect these data would be one way of drawing attention to the subject.

4 Social work provision

The roots of modern social work can be traced back to 1970 when, following the recommendations of the Seebohm Report in 1968 for a unified department, three distinct services—children, mental health and welfare—were integrated into the new social services departments. In the same year the British Association of Social Workers was created from the previously separate disciplines, and the Central Council for Education and Training in Social Work was formed from the different examining bodies. Following the attempts of social work to move towards professionalization, there was also a move towards unionization, and a national strike in 1979. A series of child care tragedies hit the headlines, causing public concern about the role of social workers, which had hitherto largely been unknown, and this signalled a period of much closer public scrutiny of the outcomes of social work intervention. In 1980 the government responded to some of these concerns by setting up an inquiry into the roles and tasks of social workers. The Barclay Report which resulted, promoted the idea of a community/patch approach to social work and re-emphasized the common base of all social work (Barclay, 1982).

Debates about the nature of social work have raged for years, and the work itself has moved towards a 'social control model' in which the role of the social worker is surveillance rather than enabling activities such as support and counselling. Public anxiety about certain groups, such as older people living alone and abused children, often appears to have been the reason behind this move. However, some see the attempt to relieve poverty and underprivilege to be the reason, and this begs the question of why society is content to provide 'apologists' for the system rather than to change the system to tackle basic inequalities.

It is important to remember that social services departments provide a broader range of services than social work and employ many different categories of staff. Residential care workers comprise the largest staff group—recent figures collected by a group working on the establishment of a professional register of social workers estimated that there were less than 30,000 social workers nationally, but 250,000 social care staff (Parker, 1990). It is also the case that the vast majority of these care staff, and of the unpaid carers in the community, are women. Over the next few years an increase in the those people living over the age of 80, coupled with the diminishing school-leaving age group, is likely to have a major impact on choices for women.

4.1 Social workers and service users

The role of social workers is, in part, defined by the legislation that gives local authorities statutory powers and responsibilities. But it is also based on a professional orientation that determines how social workers work—what their aims are and what skills and techniques they use. Professional social work skills are frequently related to communication with the service users. Take, for example, 'enabling' skills:

> Enabling activities are based on the assumption that through the process of a conversation or discussion carefully guided by the social worker, clients become better able to manage their own lives and the problems which are afflicting them.
>
> (Haines, 1975)

The form of relationship, then, is presumed and the social worker uses communication to assist the user to develop his or her life skills. But the ability to communicate is also presumed and is treated as unrelated to the user's problems. Yet it is easy to imagine how Deaf people might be included in the client group if their English language skills are poor; they are likely to confront life problems to do with housing, education, employment, health, and welfare benefits—indeed, any aspect of life which involves contact between the individual and a bureaucratic process dealing in spoken and written English. It is also easy to see that if the Deaf person is having these sorts of problems, it will be difficult for the social worker to use their 'enabling skills' because they operate through 'the process of a conversation or discussion'.

Another writer on social work skills puts the emphasis on verbal communication—the situation is presented in terms of the needs of social workers to be able to express themselves verbally:

No matter what the setting, no matter what the focus, the greater part of social work hinges on the nature and quality of relationships between workers and clients; the basic tool in such relationships, particularly in the initial stages, consists of verbal contributions by the worker and verbally expressed reactions by him (*sic*) to the client.

(Davies, 1981)

Many of the skills listed as being part of social work involve communication both with the service user and with others; for example, in counselling, social advocacy, social skills training, and assessment. In spite of this there is little reference or significance given to any mode of communication other than verbal English.

Deafness is seen, by Haines at least, as one of a group of disabilities or deficiencies that create communication problems and therefore relationship problems:

> ... it is not always realistic for social workers to expect the kind of responses that indicate that their offer of a relationship is welcome. Some clients are unable to indicate much of a response by reason of handicap or disease. Examples of this are some of those who are mentally retarded, deaf, mentally disordered or suffering senile deterioration.

(Haines, 1975)

This advice presents deafness as a problem that is not dealt with either by learning an appropriate sign language or by introducing an interpreter. It is difficult to imagine a very subtle relationship being built up between social worker and service user through an interpreter; it is not always a subtle relationship that is needed most—for the Deaf person it is often the interpretation that is really of more importance.

Deaf people have remained a 'special' client group within social work even in the Seebohm Report which argued for the introduction of generic social work. This seems at least partly because of the particular facility with sign language that was needed for social work with Deaf people. But Deaf people have gradually been seen as having different needs from other client groups, needs that are related to their different culture and their requirement for someone to act as a go-between with the dominant speaking/hearing culture.

In 1975 the Central Council for Education and Training in Social Work published a report entitled *People With Handicaps Need Better Trained Workers* (CCETSW, 1975). The report argued that all social work students should learn about different types of disability, including deafness. It also suggested that the skills needed to work with people with disabilities were essentially the same as working with other people—with two exceptions. These were that social workers with the blind and Deaf needed special training. Social Workers with Deaf People would need training in 'alternative modes of communication' and 'manual communication methods' and would also need to understand the nature of the 'handicap', including 'the implications of being born deaf and how being cut off, as a result, from normal language developments, profoundly affects the ways in which an individual develops and thinks' (CCETSW, 1975). These features would affect how assessments would be made and what resources, including residential care, would be appropriate.

◄ Activity 5
You may find it interesting to find out for yourself whether your local council makes special provision for profoundly Deaf people using its services. Are council proceedings translated into sign language? What grant support does it offer to deaf organizations?

Are there social workers for the Deaf employed by the council? ◄

◄ Comment
You may find that there are prepared written statements on the provision of services for disabled people—they may or may not distinguish services for Deaf people. If documents such as these are not available you may be relying on what an official tells you from what he or she can remember. You should find out from the education department about where their schools or units for deaf children are and how many home teachers for the deaf there are. You may also be told about sign language courses offered through the adult education section.

There is a national decline in the provision of specialist social workers for the Deaf. They are sometimes being replaced by interpreting services and staff dealing primarily with environmental aids.

New legislation on community care provision, going through parliament while this course was being prepared, will alter services for disabled people although not necessarily make any difference for most deaf people. ◄

4.2 A bridge between cultures

The Barclay Report of 1982 marks a shift away from the casework model, so bound up as it was with skills like 'enabling' and counselling in which the aim of social work was in developing a special communication with the service user. Now, less emphasis was to be put on communication as an end in itself and more on the practical problems faced by the client and how the social worker might help with these.

This shift in the orientation of social work in general has been accompanied by a critique and review of the role of social work with Deaf people. As you learnt earlier, the origins of social work with the Deaf lie in the church missions, and its history has involved strong links with the voluntary sector. The role of the Social Worker with Deaf People can be seen as a bridge between two cultures. In a now 'outmoded' role these social workers acted as go-betweens, translating and acting as agents for deaf people. Now they are seen increasingly as agents of integration, enabling 'more deaf or hard of hearing people to function without a protective and often restrictive system of care and thus share in and contribute to the riches of a wider society' (DHSS, 1988).

In recent years, the way that deaf people are seen with regard to state services has begun to change. The model of Deaf people as disabled that is enshrined in the legislation has been challenged, so that the needs of Deaf people as a cultural group with a distinct language can be addressed.

◄ Reading
You should read the models of social work with Deaf people in Article 7.2, 'Deaf People, Ethnic Minorities and Social Policy' by George Taylor, and in Article 7.3, 'The State, Social Work and Deafness' by David Parratt and Brenda Tipping in Reader Two, and consider the different ways in which these articles perceive deaf people. ◄

Hynes (1988) picks up similar themes to Taylor, encouraging a shift of social work for Deaf people away from interpretation and the supply of environmental aids. But he is cautious about altering the role of the Social Worker with Deaf People too rapidly. To do so might be to the disadvantage of those Deaf people who, because of their history of cultural isolation, continue to need direct support even if their problems are at root to do with communication. Hynes also argues that different professional services need to work more closely together in providing for Deaf people. He points out that whereas the medical profession has seen deafness as a *physical* problem, social workers have seen it as a *social* problem. But:

> There has been a particular divide between teachers and social workers. Teachers have seen social workers as putting so much emphasis on sign language and the deaf community that they are in danger of depriving deaf children of the opportunity and motivation to learn to speak, and social workers have seen teachers as putting so much emphasis on speech that they have been depriving them of access to a language in which they can communicate fluently and without pressure (BSL).
>
> (Hynes, 1988)

This describes neatly how deafness is constructed differently by the two professions. In both perspectives Deaf people are perceived as dependent and in need of professional support, but the nature of their dependence and their need for support is viewed very differently.

4.3 Legislation

You may recall that, in the list of objectives at the start of this unit, we wished to introduce you to broader policy areas. Legislation underpins all social policy and so it is important for you to be aware of the current legislation. This is listed in the *Legislation Booklet* for easy reference. One of the consequences of coming within the provisions of welfare legislation or the definition of special provision, is that the local authority had to keep records on the individual. Under the Education Act 1981, the education authority had to keep a 'statement' about the special educational needs of children assessed as having such needs (see the *Legislation Booklet*). There are rules about the sharing of information in statements with parents that cover disagreements and appeals. In other words, being recognized as having needs under the Act involves the child's parents in a bureaucratic process in which a set of records are kept on the child in a different way from those kept on other children. These pieces of legislation define a particular relationship between the state and deaf people. This relationship is not without internal contradictions and is open to a range of policy interpretations.

A more recent piece of legislation, the Disabled Persons (Services, Consultation and Representation) Act 1986, may provide an opportunity for all groups of disabled people to have some say in the types of service that local authorities offer and provide. There is provision for those seeking help from the local authority appointment of an authorized representative who may act for them or just help them in their dealings with the authority.

There is also the requirement in instances in which the disabled person is unable to communicate orally or in writing, for the provision of 'such services' as are necessary for the authority to 'discharge their functions' and so that the person is not prevented from 'the making of representations'. These provisions would enable Deaf people to appoint hearing representatives to assist them in negotiating with a bureaucracy in a language that was not their usual language. It would also mean that interpreters could be appointed to assist in the process, if necessary. At the time of writing, however (July, 1990), these Sections of the Act have yet to be implemented, which means they are advisory and not mandatory for local authorities.

A further piece of legislation to be implemented in October 1991 is the Children Act 1989 which is designed to rationalize a number of statutes relating to children and covers the responsibilities of local authorities in relation to children. In particular, the Act addresses those services for children that take over the provision of care and parental responsibility. Among other things that may affect deaf children (and other children) is the introduction of 'education supervision orders'. These appoint a designated education authority to ensure that the child receives proper education suitable to his or her age, ability and aptitude and to any special educational needs he or she may have. These educational supervision orders may only be made when a child of compulsory school age is not being properly educated. Such orders are applied for by the education authority—it is a way of giving them responsibility for the child's education when the parent is not seen to be doing the best for the child in the eyes of that authority and the court. The Children Act also puts on local authorities a responsibility to provide services for children in 'need'—those in need include disabled children. The definition of 'disabled' continues to follow that of the National Assistance Act 1948; that is, that a child is disabled 'if he is blind, deaf or dumb or suffers from mental disorder of any kind or is substantially and permanently handicapped by illness, injury or congenital deformity or such other disability as may be prescribed'.

5 Back to the future

In 1988 Sir Roy Griffiths completed a report commissioned by the government on the funding and organization of community care services for elderly and disabled people. It was entitled *Community Care: Agenda for Action* (HMSO, 1988). Griffiths' enquiry was prompted by an Audit Commission report about the levels of and arrangements for central, local and health authority funding for elderly and disabled people in residential and hospital care. In 1989 the government published a White Paper in response to the recommendations in the Griffiths Report, entitled *Caring for People: Community Care in the Next Decade and Beyond* (HMSO, 1989a). The National Health Service and Community Care Act 1990 enacts the policy laid out in the White Paper. Local authorities are required to publish plans for the provision of community care services in their areas.

How might the implementation of community care affect deaf and hard of hearing people and their rights to self-determination, equality and independence? Will it enhance their position or marginalize it?

> *Community care means providing the right level of intervention and support to enable people to achieve maximum independence and control over their own lives.*
>
> (HMSO, 1989a, p. 9)

Care in the community can be seen as part of a general social philosophy that seeks a different approach to the way that the welfare of citizens is organized. This social philosophy is reflected in other pieces of recent legislation, such as the Disabled Persons (Services, Consultation and Representation) Act 1986, the Local Government and Housing Act 1989 and the Children Act 1989, as well as in social policy reviews such as those chaired by Sir Roy Griffiths and Lady Wagner (on residential care).

Services for deaf and hard of hearing people are delivered through the social welfare structure, of which these pieces of legislation are a part. This means that, although the vast majority of deaf and hard of hearing people already live in the community, the basic principles of this philosophy, and the arrangements made to implement it, will also apply to them.

This philosophy seeks to enhance individuals' rights and freedom and their choice and control over the way their needs are met. It emanates, though, from two, sometimes conflicting, sources. One seeks to emphasize individual responsibility for personal welfare and looks for ways to reduce the size and scope of publicly financed, universally available, collective provision for the welfare of citizens. It has as its constituency the perceived needs of *all* tax payers and the need to create markets for goods and services.

The other affirms the requirement for social responsibility for the promotion of personal welfare. It seeks to develop a needs-based welfare service, which has a greater flexibility in providing for needs than exists in present arrangements and to increase the rights of people who are elderly or who are disabled, to design and obtain the services they need, via a service framework based on public subscription. It has as its constituency the perceived needs of elderly and disabled people and the need to reinforce social structures for the benefit of individuals.

Both of these sources are evident in the Griffiths Report and in the White Paper, and they both give rise to practice policies that highlight user involvement and consumer choice, the expansion of the range of services available to people by enlarging the independent sector, the monitoring of the quality of services and their cost-effectiveness, and more effective targeting of resources. The government, through the White Paper and the National Health Service and Community Care Act, has made clear its belief in the primacy of the perceived needs of tax payers and this will determine the tenor and scope of the enacted community care programme and its place in the priorities of government. This may mean that when local authorities publish community care plans that seek to promote the independent sector *in partnership* with the public sector, as both Griffiths and Wagner recommended, they may find themselves being encouraged to adjust their plans to promote the independent sector *at the expense* of the public sector.

Both Griffiths and the White Paper point to an increase in the role of the voluntary sector in providing services directly to deaf and hard of hearing people. It is also likely that this sector will become more and more predominant in direct service provision. This is a reversal of recent trends. In 1962, 79 per cent of local authorities had agency agreements with local voluntary organizations to provide services to deaf people. In 1978, only 22 per cent had agency agreements (Lysons, 1979).

> *The changes outlined in this White Paper are* ... *intended to give people a greater individual say in how they live their lives and the services they need to help them to do so.*
>
> **(HMSO, 1989a, p. 4)**

Specialized voluntary organizations could give a greater opportunity for user representation and influence on policy than do more bureaucratic and generalist public agencies which are accountable to a wider constituency. As the role of voluntary organizations increases, so too can the influence that Deaf and hard of hearing people have on the services that are provided to them. There are two issues that should be considered here. First, voluntary organizations are encouraged by the policy of community care to provide *contracted* services. These are likely to be subject to ministerial direction and to monitoring by the Social Services Inspectorate, neither of which sources are subject to local political accountability. Used appropriately, this direction and monitoring could increase user representation and control; however, they may equally be used to restrict that representation when it conflicts with the interests of government.

Second, most voluntary organizations are likely to be registered charities. Charity law in the UK does not allow beneficiaries of services provided by a charity (i.e. users) to be appointed or elected to the Board of Trustees of a charity. The charity trustees remain, as far as the law is concerned, the makers of policy. No intermediate committee or board can have anything other than an advisory function.

> *Voluntary organizations may need to make major changes in their working methods* ...
>
> **(HMSO, 1989a, p. 24)**

Voluntary organizations have for some time had important functions in campaigning, advocacy and information giving. These are largely in relation to helping people to understand what services are available and supporting them in their efforts to obtain those they have a right to receive. What happens, then, when the advisers and advocates are also the providers? Local authorities will have a responsibility to prepare plans for community care. If the voluntary sector becomes increasingly predominant in service provision, to whom do the local authorities—and deaf and hard of hearing people—go for independent advice and information? Voluntary organizations may well find themselves in the position where they are being asked to set quality standards for the services they themselves are providing, even if these are provided by charity public limited companies that are off-shoots of parent voluntary organizations.

One further critical issue also needs to be considered. As charities, voluntary organizations are constrained in their overt political activity. If services are provided more predominantly by the independent sector, not only is there a real risk of the loss of direct local political representation for deaf people, there is also a risk that services for deaf and hard of hearing people are de-politicized and taken out of the mainstream of political debate.

> *... an increasing contractural relationship ... will serve to ... enhance the development of more flexible and cost-effective forms of non-statutory provision.*
>
> **(HMSO, 1989a, p. 24)**

The voluntary sector in social services in the UK has long had a pioneering role in developing new ways of working with disabled people. As voluntary agencies become more involved in the provision of day-to-day services, this function may become more difficult to fulfil. These agencies' resources will not be unlimited and their contracts will be tight—if local authorities are able to do their job properly. Their personnel are likely to be concentrated in income-generating programmes, leading to the marginalization of developmental and innovative work. It may well be that the establishment of new small-scale bodies, as envisaged by the White Paper, will help to ensure the continuation of this type of work. These small agencies may not, however, have the necessary resources to undertake major innovative projects and will be dependent on discretionary grant aid for their survival.

> *The government recognises that its proposals will have an impact on the way in which managers and staff at all levels of the social services workforce carry out their work.*
>
> **(HMSO, 1989a, p. 67)**

Community care is going to have a major impact on the way that social workers practice. One of the key features of the policy of community care, promoted both by Griffiths and by the government, is the separation of assessment and service provision. The Disabled Persons (Services, Consultation and Representation) Act also introduces a third separated element, that of representation and information giving. This separation of functions is intended to enhance the interests of users, by giving them access to independent advocacy services, and to allow the local authority to monitor the quality of service provision on their behalf. A number of issues arise in relation to service provision for deaf and hard of hearing people.

If the assessment of need is separated from the provision of a service to meet that need, who should do the assessment? It could be undertaken by a specialist Social Worker with Deaf People or by a generic social worker using an interpreter, employed by the assessing agency. Alternatively, it could be done by independent social workers, unattached to either assessing authorities or service-providing agencies, as some Guardian Ad Litem reports are compiled or, increasingly, social enquiry reports in the Probation Service. If these functions are not separated, then assessments become service-based rather than needs-based. In other words, assessments are made in terms of what services are available, rather than what needs the person being assessed has.

If information giving and representation functions are separated from the assessing authority, can they be placed with the service-providing agency, without adversely affecting the rights and interests of potential users of a service? Some local authorities are already placing information services, under the provision of the Disabled Persons (Services, Consultation and Representation) Act, with small local groups of disabled people. These groups have no service provision responsibilities and can offer independent advice and representation to potential users about both assessment and service provision.

Finally, and perhaps of more significance than either of these two issues, there is the way that the role of social workers, whether with deaf people or hearing people, may change. At one level, the policy of community care will introduce new ways of working. The introduction of case management will, as the White Paper points out, require the development of social workers' assessment and counselling skills and will require them to learn new skills in resource management. It will also restrict the ability of social workers to act collectively with deaf people to obtain services, as the process of assessment and provision becomes more individually based. At another level, the changes may be even more dramatic. Local authorities may not wish to contract out statutory responsibilities, such as those under the Mental Health Act 1983 and the Children Act 1989. Indeed, there may be legal constraints on their ability to do this. Equally, voluntary agencies may be unwilling to bid for services that may prove more expensive and difficult to provide than flexible, non-statutory services. This could lead to the development of two tiers of workers—social workers and social care officers—with different levels of training, status and expertise. Users may not necessarily benefit from this division.

Community care has the capacity to create opportunities for the development of services for deaf and hard of hearing people and the enhancement of their rights and interests. There is, however, also a danger that services will become marginalized, non-accountable and monopolistic, to the detriment of users. The key lies in which constituency of perceived need takes precedent in setting the guidelines for the provision of services—the needs of elderly and disabled people and the development of collective support networks, or the needs of tax payers and the development of markets. Much will then depend on the type and variety of organizations that are set up to carry out the different functions of community care. If a number of independent organizations can be established, then it may be possible to achieve the separation of function envisaged by the government's policy. However, there is one key difficulty and this concerns the nature of these organizations. Charity-based agencies may inhibit the development of proper user representation and the ability of organizations to engage in open political activity on behalf of their clients. The government's recent White Paper on charity reform, *Charities: A Framework for the Future* (HMSO, 1989b), does not address this issue. Any new form of incorporated body, such as charitable companies, will owe their primary duty to 'particular charitable purposes', and so will remain within the charitable framework. It would see that the government's much heralded wish to enable people to 'achieve ... control over their lives' does not include their ability to exercise political power.

Ultimately, then, deaf and hard of hearing people who use services may continue to be denied the opportunity to create policy and to decide what services they require to enable them to achieve their rights of independence, equality and self-determination.

6 Conclusion

You will remember that, in the Introduction to this unit, a number of themes were referred to which would be mentioned throughout. In concluding this unit we return to some of these. First, the fact that legislation and service provision fails to acknowledge Deaf people as a distinct group is apparent in the most recent legislation also, and deafness is assumed to be dealt with within disability. This seems unlikely to change substantially in the foreseeable future. However, there are some early signs which could turn out to be positive. All the most recent Acts place much emphasis on consultation with service users and whilst this is no easy solution, it is one area in which the strength of the Deaf community could produce results. Also, recent legislation stresses the need for service providers to provide information, and in an accessible form. This opens up further possibilities and once again Deaf clubs could be a useful network for sharing information.

You will remember a reference in Section 1 to the role of the early missioners, and later the influence that social workers have in many Deaf people's lives. It is worth considering whether this is likely to continue if other professional groups and agencies see the need to make their own services accessible. The power of Social Workers with Deaf People would perhaps then be reduced to the level of their generic colleagues, which is still powerful indeed.

Social Workers with Deaf People are the only group to have accepted the need for sign language skills as a matter of course and the recent developments in separating out interpreting tasks may at present be the most significant trend. This may, of course, result in generic social workers using interpreters, which we have argued against. Alternatively, it may mean that the majority of Deaf people would not be caught in the 'welfare net' as they could conduct their lives independently using interpreters when required. This would leave the minority, who do require social work and social services, with a better staffed service which should be able to meet their needs more adequately.

Suggestions for further reading

There are many books about the development and practice of social work. If you are interested in reading further, a good one to consult is:
DAVIES, M. (1981) *The Essential Social Worker, A Guide to Positive Practice*, London, Heinemann.

Little has been written about the practice of social work with deaf people. A monograph providing a general introduction to the issues is:
HYNES, D. (1988) *Social Work with Deaf People*, Social Work Monographs, Norwich, University of East Anglia.

The 1988 DHSS report *Say It Again* looked at social work practices with Deaf people. While it reviewed the position current at that time, many were disappointed that it was not more radical in its proposals:
DHSS, SOCIAL SERVICES INSPECTORATE (1988) *'Say It Again:' Contemporary Social Work Practices with People Who are Deaf or Hard of Hearing*, London, Social Services Inspectorate, Department of Health and Social Security.

References

BARCLAY, P. (1982) *Social Workers: Their Roles and Their Tasks, the Report of a Working Party Set Up by the National Institute of Social Work at the Request of the Secretary of State for Social Services*, London, NISW.

BRIEN, D. (1981) *Is There a Deaf Culture Available to the Deaf Young Person?* NCSWD. (An excerpt from this is included in Reader Two.)

CACDP (1985) *Council for the Advancement of Communication with Deaf People, Register of Interpreters, Code of Practice*, Durham, CACDP/RID, April 1985.

CCETSW (1975) *People With Handicaps Need Better Trained Workers*, London, Central Council for Education and Training in Social Work.

CCETSW (1989) *Requirements and Regulations for the Diploma in Social Work: Paper 30,* London, Central Council for Education and Training in Social Work.

DAVIES, M. (1981) *The Essential Social Worker: Guide to Positive Practice*, London, Heinemann.

DEPARTMENT OF HEALTH, SOCIAL SERVICES INSPECTORATE (1989) *'A Secret Service': An Evaluation of PSS for People With Hearing Impairment in Tameside*, London, Social Services Inspectorate, Department of Health.

DHSS, SOCIAL SERVICES INSPECTORATE (1988) *'Say It Again': Contemporary Social Work Practice with People Who Are Deaf or Hard of Hearing*, London, Social Services Inspectorate, Department of Health and Social Security.

DHSS, SOCIAL WORK SERVICE (1977) The Advisory Committee on Services for Hearing Impaired People, London, Department of Health and Social Security.

EICHHOLZ REPORT (1932) *Eichholz Report: A Study of the Deaf in England and Wales 1930–32*, London, HMSO.

FINKELSTEIN, V. (1990) ' "We" are not disabled, "you" are', in Gregory, S. and Hartley, G.M. (eds) (1990) *Constructing Deafness*, London, Pinter Publishers. (D251 Reader Two, Article 7.6)

FIRTH, G. (1989) *Chosen Vessels: A Tribute to Those Pioneers in the Care of the Deaf*, Exeter, published by the author.

GREGORY, S. and HARTLEY, G. (eds) (1990) *Constructing Deafness*, London, Pinter Publishers. (D251 Reader Two)

HAINES, J. (1975) *Skills and Methods in Social Work*, London, Constable.

HMSO (1988) *Community Care: Agenda for Action* (The Griffiths Report), London, HMSO.

HMSO (1989a) *Caring For People: Community Care in the Next Decade and Beyond*, Government White Paper, London, HMSO.

HMSO (1989b) *Charities: A Framework For the Future*, CM 694, London, HMSO.

HYNES, D. (1988) *Social Work with Deaf People*, Social Work Monographs, Norwich, University of East Anglia.

KEOGAN, T. (1986) *Document for Management Discussion on Services for the Deaf, Deaf/Blind and Hearing Impaired*, Cleveland, Social Services Department.

KING, J. (1990) 'Free expression', *Community Care* Supplement, 26 April.

KYLE, J. (1986) 'Deaf people and minority groups in the UK', in Gregory, S. and Hartley, G.M. (eds) (1990) *Constructing Deafness*, London, Pinter Publishers. (D251 Reader Two, Article 7.7)

LYSONS, C.K. (1965) *Voluntary Welfare Societies for Adult Deaf Persons in England 1940–63*, MA Thesis, London, Royal National Institute for the Deaf.

LYSONS, C.K. (1979) *The Development of Local Voluntary Societies for Adult Deaf Persons in England*, Carlisle, The British Deaf Association. (Also Article 7.1 in D251 Reader Two.)

MOORHEAD, D. (1990) 'Social work and interpreting', in Gregory, S. and Hartley, G.M. (eds) (1990) *Constructing Deafness*, London, Pinter Publishers. (D251 Reader Two, Article 7.5)

PAGEL, M. (1988) *On Our Own Behalf*, Manchester, Greater Manchester Coalition of Disabled People.

PARKER, R. (1990) 'Social work register call', *The Guardian*, 24 March.

PARRATT, D. and TIPPING, B. (1986) 'The state, social work and deafness', in Gregory, S. and Hartley, G.M. (eds) (1990) *Constructing Deafness*, London, Pinter Publishers. (D251 Reader Two, Article 7.3)

PECKFORD, R. and HAWCROFT, L. (1990) 'Needles in haystacks', *Community Care*, 16 August.

RILEY, T.A. (1988) *A Consumer's Point of View*, Paper to the European Sign Language Interpreters Conference, October, Scotland.

RNID (1987) *So Little for So Many*, Survey of Provision to Hearing Impaired People by Social Services Departments, London, Royal National Institute for the Deaf.

RNID (1988) *Is There Anybody Listening?*, Survey of Staff Employed in England to Provide Social Services for Deaf People, Research Report No. 4, London, Royal National Institute for the Deaf.

SCOTT-GIBSON, L. (1990) 'Sign language interpreting: an emerging profession', in Gregory, S. and Hartley, G.M. (eds) (1990) *Constructing Deafness*, London, Pinter Publishers. (D251 Reader Two, Article 7.4)

SEEBOHM REPORT (1968) Report of the Committee on Local Authority and Allied Personal Social Services, London, HMSO.

SIMPSON, T.S. (1990) 'A stimulus to learning, a measure of ability', in Gregory, S. and Hartley, G.M. (eds) (1990) *Constructing Deafness*, London, Pinter Publishers. (D251 Reader Two, Article 6.6)

STEVENSON, O. (1981) *Specialisation in Social Service Teams*, London, Allen and Unwin.

TAYLOR, G. (1986) 'Deaf people, ethnic minorities and social policy', in Gregory, S. and Hartley, G.M. (eds) (1990) *Constructing Deafness*, London, Pinter Publishers. (D251 Reader Two, Article 7.2)

YOUNGHUSBAND REPORT (1959) Report of the Working Party on Social Work in Local Authority Health and Welfare Services, London, HMSO.

Acknowledgement

Grateful acknowledgement is made to Trevor Landell for permission to use his painting on the covers and title pages throughout the units of this course.